PRAISE FOR MINOUDE GUSTAVE

I was delighted when Minoude asked me to write about her. It is my honor to express my wholehearted support for Minoude in this emotional journey. Although Minoude and I have gone to the same church, I came to truly know her when we started attending the New York School of Ministry about two years ago. I remember that faithful Saturday morning, when we started our first ministry course. What was supposed to be a short day, where both of us were thinking of dropping out of the program, turned out to be an awesome opportunity to continue to excel and to eventually become Ministers of the Gospel, as the Lord sees fit.

Minoude is a friend, sister, and prayer partner. She is a woman of few words, but always speaks volume on the most sensitive subjects of our time. Looking through this magnificent book, I am absolutely amazed at Minoude's talents, and what she has achieved with her pencil. Minoude's story is unique, but resonates with every generation. There is something for everyone in Minoude's life story. Please read and enjoy this phenomenal book and learn from it. It is more than a book on abandonment, distrust, pain, but also a delightful illustration of love, hope, and most of all, friendship.

May God bless you in all your future endeavors. The sky is the limit Minoude. Keep the faith. The best is yet to come.

-Love Always, Your friend, sister, prayer partner, GUETHY LEDAN

My Aunt Minoude, whom I will be referring to as Auntie in this insert, is one of the most inspiring people I know. Growing up around her, I've seen both the best and the worst sides of her. Despite her flaws, her greatness always shone through for me. Now, as an adult, I can say she truly is one of my best friends and a confidant. The truth is, I've always felt safe around her, even as a child.

The first time I was unknowingly left home alone, I didn't think to call anyone else but her. As the true Auntie she is, even though she couldn't afford it at the time, she sacrificed getting a cab to come get me so that I would be safe. Although it didn't get that far, knowing that I had someone to save me kept me calm until someone else got home.

Auntie has taught me a lot about life through her successes and failures and has truly been a mentor for me since the age of 16. Learning how she overcame her struggles and never showed us (my cousin and me) that she was truly struggling was admirable to me. Aside from the values my parents instilled in me, watching someone go through and get through what my aunt has been through allowed me to see not only her strength but also that if you don't let anything stop you from succeeding in life, you will always arrive at where you want to be.

Auntie has always been a progressive person, but I can truly say that seeing and watching her grow exponentially over the last three years is still somewhat unbelievable to me. It's a blessing to witness firsthand how discipline and determination can propel someone's life in such a short amount of time. She's always displayed these characteristics, but when God revealed to her what her true purpose in life is, she moved swiftly and fearlessly as a true obedient disciple to receive the best that He had in store for her.

Although her story does not end here, I'm still super amazed at the transformations she's made and beyond proud of how much she's grown spiritually, emotionally, and mentally as a woman. I've always felt that her story should be told and shown to the world because it feels like a testimony that others need to hear, so they too can see and know that where you are today does not mean that's where you'll be tomorrow.

Now, the world gets to see the side of her that I've always known, but they're even luckier than I am because it's in one book, whereas I had to witness it over almost 30 years of living. Honestly, I could write a book about our relationship, and it would probably be the size of a textbook, but I'll end it here.

I wish you nothing but success, peace, and happiness as you continue to grow into the woman God wants you to be. I love you to pieces, and congratulations on the release of your first book!

-DIANNE RAEBURN

Hard as nails on the outside but sweet and soft on the inside. Look and read the selfless journey of her life. See the blessings that God has bestowed on her. Read about the gifts that God has given her and the blessings she shares with others.

Bless you and continue your journey with God. Minoude Gustave. What can you say about Minoude. She's a quiet storm. A sweet quiet passionate storm that builds and grows to its crescendo and envelope you into her being if she allows it. All business when business is called for pulls no punches and knows how to gently place your back on the mat. Minoude is soft-spoken; someone you don't see coming, but when something isn't right and clarification is needed, Minoude has a mighty voice. She's perfected putting those strong words on paper, and when she does, you must pay attention. She lands every punch thrown with precision. There is no malice in what she says or does. Only what needs to be said at that time and nothing more, she is true to herself and others. Very personable and warm. Give her what she asks for and Minoude becomes an individual you want on your side. Congratulations on your first publication with many more to come.

-BERNADETTE SAMUEL, RN MSN, Clinical Professional Development Educator

Witty, smart, dedicated, strong, and caring, are just a few words to describe Minoude. We met almost three years ago now through a mutual friend at church. Over time, we grew close, and I have had the privilege of witnessing firsthand how God has transformed Minoude's life. For a season, the Lord used Minoude to minister to me in a miraculous way, but little did she know that God was preparing her for what was to come in her own life. She is a person who wants to see others well, and she will do whatever she can to support you. Minoude embodies Proverbs 27:17, which reads, "As iron sharpens iron, so a friend sharpens a friend," NLT. I'm so honored to have her in my life because I believe God put us in each other's lives for such a time as this.

Minoude, my sister, I am so proud of you. This is only the beginning, may God continue to do a mighty work in and through you.

With love,

MONICA MTONGA-ANDERSON, Founder of You Are Kingdom Woman Ministries

I CAN SEE THE LIGHT

A Journey of Faith and Transformation

MINOUDE GUSTAVE

Cover Design by John Bryll Pulido; website : brilliantcover.com

Formatted by Ruth L. Snyder

Paperback: 978-1-998542-00-0

Ebook: 978-1-998542-01-7

DEDICATION

I dedicate this book to all those who find themselves without a voice, to the ones who may feel unheard or unseen. May these words serve as a reminder that in the eyes of God, you are significant. Remember, He has a purpose for your life, and in Him, you will find the strength and guidance to navigate your journey. Look to the heavens for solace, seek His wisdom in times of need, and witness the miraculous ways in which He will manifest His power in your life.

CONTENTS

Introduction   xv

1. The Root of My Faith   1
2. Life in America   7
3. Single Parenting and Dating   17
4. Picking Up the Pieces   25
5. The Struggle Continues   31
6. A Glimmer of Light   43
7. One Last Fight   57
8. Forgiveness   61
9. What in the World?   65
10. My Relationships   71
11. Looking Ahead   75

Afterword   77
About the Author   79

INTRODUCTION

I have been a Christian all my life. I remember attending church and prayer meetings with my grandmother at a very young age. When I lived with my grandparents our daily routine included prayers and reading the Bible daily. Everyone in our household recited Psalm 23 and the Lord's Prayer together as a family. When I became a teenager, I was in and out of the church, however, I never stopped praying and reciting Psalm 23. In my early 20s, I started attending church regularly. However, it wasn't until 2010 that I gave my life to Christ and was water-baptized in early 2011. My church attendance was good, and I participated in a lot of different small groups and other church events. Many times, in my life even though I was a follower of Christ, I still had a lot of fleshy ways.

One of the pastors from my church transferred to a new church where he was the lead pastor. I decided to go visit his church and it was in that church that I began to feel like I found my home church. I was not looking for a new church, however, God had revealed to me that this would be my new church, and I decided to stay. As I met different people in the church and built relationships, I wanted more. In October 2021, I decided to break up with my boyfriend and get rid of everything that came between me and my relationship with God. My prayer life changed drastically, and I just wanted more of God; I wanted a deeper relationship with my Creator. I was the happiest that I have ever been, and I was able to build new friendships. Then I realized that I spent all my life looking for love and friendships in all the wrong places. I began to ask God to change me.

January 2022 was the church's annual 21-day fast (3 weeks). My only goal for this fast was to grow closer to God. I wanted a better relationship with Him, and I wanted to build new and genuine friendships with like-minded people. I wanted to be part of a ministry but was looking to God for guidance and direction. During the first week of the fast, I felt discouraged, I was stressed out, and I felt like God was far from me. I kept going because I knew the enemy did not want me to succeed. On day 15, we were instructed to pray for a partner (husband/wife). I prayed for a husband and everything that I wanted in a husband, and it didn't take long before God showed me in a dream that He was going to send me a husband. This is someone I had seen in person, and although we had not officially met, I had seen him in the church.

Now fast forward to April 2022, I became impatient and wanted to know why I hadn't met my future husband yet. It's not like God to show me something that did not come to pass, for it says in Isaiah 55:11 "So is my word that goes from my mouth: It will not return to me empty but will accomplish what I desire and achieve the purpose for which I sent it." I wanted to hear from God. I needed confirmation. I decided to do a one-day fast to ask God why this man hadn't approached me yet. That night after the one-day fast, God came to me in a vision and told me that I was not ready for what he had planned for me and that I needed to heal first. Wait, what? I needed to what? But God, I thought I was healed.

I forgave whom I needed to forgive; I made peace with everyone/everything, or so I thought. God instructed me to start writing about my life, because this would be where I would find complete healing.

I began to write about my life. I thought it would be a breeze. Boy oh boy, was I wrong. I started to remember things from my childhood that I hadn't thought about for many years. Some were very emotional for me; I was becoming very sad. I shared what I was experiencing with someone in the church, and she advised me to talk to somebody, a therapist. I began my search for a therapist, and I found a therapist within that same week. Three weeks into therapy, God revealed to me some of the areas where I needed to heal. I am looking forward to being completely healed and I am excited to see what God has planned for my future.

Chapter One

THE ROOT OF MY FAITH

"The Lord is my shepherd, I lack nothing."
Psalm 23:1

I was born in Port Au Prince Haiti, a country in the Caribbean Sea that includes the western third of the island of Hispaniola. My mother was a single parent of two: my older sister and me. My mother traveled frequently to the U.S. and other countries and eventually settled in the U.S. My sister and I were sent to Jacmel to live with our grandparents and our aunts.

Jacmel is a port town on the south coast of Haiti. I was 3 years old when we were sent to Jacmel however, I don't have any memories of living with my mother until I came to the U.S. when I was twelve years old. My experience living in Jacmel was great, especially when my grandfather was alive. He was the first man I ever loved; he was more of a father to me than my own father.

My grandparents had ten children: seven girls and three boys. My mother was number three. My grandfather was a farmer who owned a lot of land. He was a very hard-working man, and my grandmother was a home-maker. Living in Jacmel was the closest I came to living a normal life. We had our daily routine of Bible reading and prayer together as a family.

My father came to visit a couple of times, however, there was no quality time spent together. My grandfather spent a lot of time with us. My fondest memory of my grandfather was when he used to chase after my grandmother to stop her from catching us when we were running away from her when we were in trouble. This would turn into playtime because my sister and I would start laughing so hard that my grandmother would start laughing as well and eventually stop chasing us.

My grandfather did a lot of funny things to make us laugh. He was the best grandfather. My worst experience was my grandfather's untimely death. One night my grandfather did not come home. It was not like him to stay out and not come home. My grandmother was frantically looking for him everywhere. I was worried about him that night and I prayed that he was okay.

The next morning, we woke up to find my grandfather hanging on a tree on the side of the house. This was the most devastating thing that I have ever experienced in my life. Later that night, someone came to me in a dream to tell me what happened to my grandfather. He did not commit suicide. My grandfather was murdered because of jealousy over his possessions.

I had a tough time understanding why someone would do that to my grandfather. I could not process my grandfather being gone; I was between the ages of 5 and 7 when my grandfather passed away. After my grandfather's funeral, my family was not very kind to me. They were very judgmental towards me for not crying at the funeral. Because I had a very close relationship with my grandfather, they were expecting more reactions from me. I was in a state of shock. I just shut down. I did not know how to process everything; I was just a child.

I was never the same after the passing of my grandfather. When my mother came to visit us in Haiti, my sister would cry and beg her to stay, and I would just say my goodbyes and go about my day. To my family, I was considered cold and heartless. They did not possess the tools to recognize that I was grieving my grandfather. They did not realize people react differently to trauma. I was a child; I did not know what to do with what I was feeling.

Life in Jacmel was different after my grandfather passed. I lived there for an additional 2-3 years before we were sent back to Port Au Prince to live with my father and my aunt. My father was never home. He left the house early in the morning and returned home late at night, and he never really spent quality time with us. It felt as if he only came home to eat, shower, and sleep.

My aunt was hired to take care of my sister and me. My aunt was physically abusive to us, beating us multiple times per day. She was very mean to us. I remember one time when she was beating me and blood was gushing out of an unhealed wound from a previous beating, and that did not stop her from beating me. She beat me with extension cords, leather belts, tree branches, leather whips, and anything she could get her hands on. She made me kneel on a cheese grater covered with uncooked rice, as a punishment. My father was oblivious to all the abuse that was going on in the house. My father saw my legs with open wounds and scars, but he never cared enough to ask how I got them.

In addition to physical abuse, I endured sexual molestation while I was living in Port au Prince with my aunt and father. Unfortunately, I did not know back then that's what it was. I did not know if there was a name for it, or if people could get in trouble when caught until I was in my mid-20s living in America. A family friend who used to take us to church every Sunday was molesting me. He would kiss me on the lips and touch me in inappropriate places. He was in his late 20s and early 30s, and he seemed nice at the time.

I didn't know that what he was doing was wrong. We were never taught to report these things to an adult, and people didn't talk about these things. Children were to be seen, not heard, and if I did tell, no one would have believed me over an adult.

I was also molested by a female, another friend of the family. She was over 18 years old when she molested me.

She would touch me inappropriately and she would stick her finger into my private area. Two guys from the neighborhood grocery store also molested me. They kissed me on the lips with their tongues and touched me in inappropriate places, they were at least in their 20s. Life in Port Au Prince was daily beating and molestation. It was different from the life I had in Jacmel with my grandparents.

I was taught children were not allowed to express their feelings; children could not look at adults in the eyes when they were speaking as it was considered disrespectful. I was molested multiple times by multiple people, and no one came to my rescue.

I was also taught any adult could discipline any child as they saw fit. God forbid you were acting out in the street and a surrounding neighbor saw you, because they would discipline you and tell your parents/guardian. Then when you arrived home your parents/guardian would discipline you as well.

Those nosy neighbors never saw me getting molested, but somehow if I was misbehaving, they would see that. I never realized how those events affected my life until I was in my mid to late 20s.

Chapter Two

LIFE IN AMERICA

"He makes me lie down in green pastures."
Psalm 23:2a

When I was 12 years old, I received the great news that I was going to the U.S. to live with my mother. I was excited and nervous at the same time because I was not sure how my mother would receive me; I did not really know her. My sister was supposed to arrive in the U.S. first, then I would follow a few months later.

My sister decided to stay in Haiti a little longer, so I ended up being first. Did I mention I was nervous? I did not know how things would be with just me and my mother as I had no memory of ever living with her. When I arrived at the airport, my mother was there to pick me up. I was shocked to see that she was pregnant, something I did not know before I came. In my mind, she and my father were still together.

When we arrived home from the airport, my mother introduced me to her husband, another shocker. But wait, there is more, my mother told me to call him Daddy, and she said, "When you wake up in the morning say, good morning, Daddy." I asked her what Daddy meant and she told me. From there I knew I was going to have a problem living with my mother.

As a child, I had no right to say no or even express how I felt. I tried to avoid him in the mornings so I wouldn't have to call him daddy. Sometimes I acted as if I forgot the word daddy; since I didn't speak English, it was believable.

We lived in an apartment building in Queens surrounded by drug dealers. I had to help around the house, go to the laundromat, and go grocery shopping. One day when I was coming back home from the supermarket I got on the elevator and there was a white man there. He got in the elevator with me. As the elevator door closed, he exposed himself to me.

I was terrified, but thankfully the elevator stopped on the second floor, the door opened, and I ran out of the elevator. I went home shaking. My mother asked if I was okay, but I was afraid to tell her what happened because I thought I would be in trouble. I told my mother I was okay and went straight to bed. After that incident, I was afraid to get on elevators. Even now as an adult I don't like getting on elevators.

After three long months in the U.S. with my mother and stepfather, my sister finally arrived. My sister and I are vastly different. People often compared our personalities which was very frustrating for me. I was very reserved, and I was not much of a talker. If I did not know you, it would take time for me to open up. People criticized me for my personality_family members, and friends of the family. They would say it right in front of me, "She's just like her father, she has no personality." At some point, I started to believe that I had no personality. I stayed away from people because of that. I don't think they realized how hurtful they were being. I was a child; it was their responsibility to build me up and not tear me down. I was also called the ugly one because of my darker complexion. I was at a point where I did not want to be around people because I was tired of their negative comments toward me.

When it came time to go to school, I was placed in the 6th grade and my sister was placed in the 7th grade. Within a few months of me being in the 6th grade, I was moved to the 7th grade, the same class as my sister. I am not sure about how my sister felt about that. I was the uncool little sister following her around and now we were in the same class. That must have been tough for her.

My sister enjoyed hanging out with her friends after school and we were always getting into trouble with my mother because we would go home past our curfew. We were expected to be home right after school. My sister always wanted to hang out with her friends after school. I could not go home without her but, I would get in trouble waiting for her. It was a no-win situation for me. Either way, I would be in trouble.

Every time we went home late, we would get a beating, which was every day, thanks to my sister. I grew so tired of all the beatings that I began to run away from home. When I was 14 years old, I started dating one of the drug dealers in the neighborhood. He was 19. I often ran away with him. My mom would make me go back home.

Whenever I was in trouble, my mother would beat me, and I would run away again. My mother and step-father had a weekly bingo game they attended every Saturday evening. While they were out playing bingo, my sister and I would take turns going out because one of us had to stay home with our little sister. One night they left for their bingo night, as usual. We had agreed I would go out first and then my sister would go upon my return. That night the bingo game must've been canceled; they came home while I was still out.

I was with a friend from the neighborhood. As my friend and I were approaching the door, I heard my mother screaming saying that she was going to beat me when I got home. So, I ran away again that night. My friend who was with me also ran away. We met an older gentleman in the neighborhood and asked if we could stay at his house for the night and he said we could. He was a very nice man; I think he felt sorry for us. I never realized how dangerous this could have been until later in life.

We went back home a couple of days later and I did not get a beating. However, it did not take long before I ran away again, this time accompanied by my sister. I think all immigrant parents like to threaten to send their kids back home. My mother was serious about that threat. My sister and I were scared, and we did not want to go back.

One evening we waited for my mother and stepfather to go out, then we packed some clothes into a garbage bag and left through the fire escape to avoid bumping into the landlord. He was a nosy Haitian man who always told on us. We ended up staying at my boyfriend's friend's house, another drug dealer from the neighborhood.

On the first night there, he made a pass at me. I reported his behavior to my boyfriend the next day and he took us to another friend's house in Brooklyn. After a while, my sister became homesick and wanted to go back home, so we went back.

On the first day of high school, I thought to myself "I am older now, I can stay out late." Boy was I wrong. I went home at 6 pm after school. When I arrived home my mother was there on the couch waiting for me. She said, "If you're not going to follow my rules, you can go back to where you came from." So, I went back to where I came from and never returned.

I was living in a basement apartment with my boyfriend. On my 15th birthday, I was sick—vomiting and feeling dizzy. I was not sure what was wrong with me. I was afraid to go to the hospital because I was underage, and I knew they would call my mother. My boyfriend told his mother that I was sick, and she told him to buy a pregnancy test because she thought I was pregnant. He bought the pregnancy test, and three minutes later, I discovered I was pregnant. I thought to myself, now there is no way I am returning home. I didn't want to cause any more shame and embarrassment to my mother. My boyfriend's mother asked me to have an abortion because she did not want to have a dark-skinned grandchild. I did not know what I was going to do. I would not choose abortion as an option.

My boyfriend managed to get us an apartment, and things were going well, until a few months later. While we were in bed sleeping the police/FBI kicked in the door and threw me down to the ground on my belly. I told them, "I'm pregnant. Please stop!" They did not care. They were so rough, I was crying and in pain. They took my boyfriend away and left me there by myself. I did not know what to do or where they were taking him. I was terrified.

I was friends with this girl in the building and her mother helped me find where they had taken him. He was in jail and there was nothing I could have done to help. His best friend was an informant who gave him up to the FBI to avoid jail time. You see, we lived in a bad neighborhood. Even though my boyfriend was a drug dealer, he did not carry any weapons. A few days before my boyfriend's arrest, his best friend gave him a bag full of weapons to hold for him. I didn't know about this until after my boyfriend was arrested. His own so-called best friend betrayed him.

I ended up living with my friend's mother for a little while until I was summoned to family court by my mother. When we were in court, the judge gave my mother the option to take me home or to send me to a group home for pregnant teens in the Bronx. With no hesitation, my mother said, "Send her to a group home." Granted, I did not want to go home with my mother. However, hearing her say that she did not want me to go back home with her hurt me deeply.

I can't say this was the first time I felt rejected by my mother. To me it felt like confirmation of what I had been feeling all along—that I was alone. I always felt like my mother didn't love me as much as she loved my sisters. I cried all the way to the group home and all night long that night. I resented my mother for a long time. She came to visit often and every visit she had to deal with my nasty attitude. Sometimes I didn't even want to see her.

I never cared about what it took for her to come to the Bronx to see me. She had to ask her friend to go with her and they would sometimes get lost. I just did not care. I lived in the group home for pregnant teens for the remainder of my pregnancy. There I was able to attend classes to complete the 9th grade. They had different activities and classes to help us prepare for motherhood. I never went to visit my mother and sisters in Queens because I did not want to bring any more shame to the family.

The hospital where I was going to give birth was attached to the group home, just an elevator ride away.

My due date was June 19th, on June 18th I went in the shower to get ready for bed, and after my shower, I felt my water break. One of the staff members took me to the hospital and left me there alone and did not inform my family or anyone that I was in the hospital until the following day. No one was in the hospital with me when I gave birth to my daughter.

My mother came to visit me in the hospital after my daughter was born. The director of the group home was not happy that the staff member left me there alone. It was at the end of her shift. she probably forgot to tell anyone. It didn't even matter to me because I didn't think anyone cared anyway. After I gave birth to my daughter, I had to wait an additional couple of weeks at the group home for pregnant teenagers while they were looking for a spot at another group home for teenage parents. While I was waiting for a spot, I had to leave my daughter in the hospital nursery until they found a home for us. I spent a lot of time in the hospital with my daughter. However, I was not allowed to stay overnight.

Finally, after two long weeks of waiting, they found me a spot. Within a few days, I was transferred to Brooklyn to my new home. It was a nice place fully staffed. They had everything we needed and an in-house daycare for our kids. I learned so much in that home—we had chores and other responsibilities. They gave us a weekly allowance and a monthly stipend. People from different organizations used to come and talk to us and educate us on different topics. We went on trips with and without our children and enjoyed some weekend getaways. They sent us to different shows and plays for ourselves and activities with our children.

One person oversaw cooking for the week. Whoever was assigned to cook had to create a menu for the week and she and a staff member would go to the super-market to purchase everything she would need to carry on her cooking duty for the week. We had specific staff assigned to assist in the kitchen to help and teach us how to cook. It was such an invaluable life experience for me. I was still resentful toward my mother, but that did not stop her from visiting me and participating in activities when she was invited. We celebrated every holiday, and we would perform during our Christmas holiday parties. They gave me a great foundation and I appreciated everything I learned from that house.

During my last year of high school, I did an internship at NYC BOE. I thoroughly enjoyed the experience. I wanted to work there but I was not sure if they were hiring. Towards the end of my internship, the manager called me into her office stating they had an open posi-tion for an administrative assistant and she offered the position to me. I was happy.

I worked there until I decided to go to business school. I worked hard and saved for some time and then moved out of the group home into my own apartment. I moved into a one-bedroom apartment but the neigh-borhood was not great. However, that was all I could afford at the time. My daughter's father was still in jail.

I started to visit him with my daughter, and I visited a couple of times. I didn't visit too often because I didn't enjoy going there with my daughter. We mostly communicated on the phone. He was released from jail when my daughter was 5 years old. He was only out for two weeks before he violated his parole and ended up back in jail. This time they kept him in jail for a couple of years and then deported him back to his country. It was tough because my daughter never got to spend any time with her father.

Chapter Three

SINGLE PARENTING AND DATING

"...he leads me beside quiet waters." Psalm 23:2b

Finally, I felt I was ready to date again. I went on a date with the head of safety at my job. He was 35 and I was 20 years old. I thought he was the best thing since sliced bread he was every-thing I thought I wanted. As I got older, I realized that it was not much of a relationship— this man was just taking advantage of me.

A year into the relationship, I got pregnant. I was already struggling with my one child and now I was pregnant with a second child. I called him to deliver the news, he said "I know what you are going to say, I had a dream about it last night. You're not keeping it." He further stated, "I don't even want the one that I have now." He was referring to his daughter from a previous relationship.

I was so hurt, I didn't know what to do. I called my sister to tell her what happened, and I told her I didn't want to have two kids without a father. I asked my sister to help me find a place to go to terminate the pregnancy. I was sad, crying every day. I just couldn't go through another pregnancy on my own while I was already struggling. I was making $9 per hour and when I applied for a food stamp, I did not get approved because I was making above the threshold.

The day finally came to terminate the pregnancy. I took the train to the clinic, and I was crying uncontrollably before and after the procedure. The other ladies there were looking at me as if I was crazy. The nurse asked me if I changed my mind. I wanted to change my mind but I couldn't see how I was going to take care of two kids without a father. The nurse did her best to comfort me, but nothing worked because I was heartbroken.

After the procedure, I called my boyfriend to pick me up from the clinic. He told me to take the train. I felt like garbage. To make matters worse, I found out this man had a girlfriend the whole time we were together. I was so hurt that I stopped all communication with him.

A few months later he called me to say how much he missed me, and he was no longer with his girlfriend and wanted to meet up to talk. I stupidly believed him and went to meet up with him. He talked like nothing happened, he was very nice to me, and he seemed in better spirits and of course, we ended up going home together.

A few days later, his girlfriend called me from his house. I felt so stupid and ended that failed relationship for good. I was very angry, and I stayed angry for many years. He eventually reached out to me about 12 years ago and wanted to meet. I was skeptical, but I still agreed to meet him for dinner. I was curious to know what he wanted from me.

We met at a restaurant. It started with small talk then he said, "The reason I asked to meet with you is to apologize to you for the way I've treated you. You were always very kind to me and did not deserve the way I treated you." I didn't say much, I accepted his apology then after dinner, we said goodbye. I never saw or talked to him again after that. As I mentioned earlier, my first apartment was not in a great neighborhood. My mother visited often but every time she visited, she always complained about how unsafe the neighborhood was.

I never had an issue in that neighborhood. Although there were a lot of drug dealers and drug-addicted people, nobody ever bothered me. I kept to myself. The guys used to say hello to me, and I would say hello back and go about my business. I was working in the morning and going to school in the evening for business management. My daughter was in school and after school.

My mother kept nagging me about the neighborhood, and now that my sister wasn't living with her anymore, she wanted me to move back home with her. How convenient, right? I didn't want to move in with my mother. My daughter and I had a great routine, and I had my privacy. Why would I want to give that up? My mother was relentless, to the point, I just said, "OKAY for the sake of my daughter!" I wanted my daughter to have a better life than I did.

I moved back home with my mother against my better judgment. Living with my mother started well. I was working and going to school, and I did not spend a lot of time in the house. I was dating a military guy by this time. I wanted to take things slow. However, he was moving extremely fast.

Three months into the relationship he proposed to me in public (The South Street Seaport). I said yes to save him embarrassment, but I needed to figure out how I was going to get out of that yes. A week after the proposal, he took me to a wedding planner to plan our wedding, I never saw myself getting married, let alone getting married to him. Now I was sitting with a wedding planner planning my wedding. Very scary! I did not know what to do. I just let him choose whatever he wanted. Shortly after that, I found out I was pregnant; I felt like I was stuck with him.

During my 3 months checkup, the doctor couldn't find the heartbeat and told me I had to wait until I started bleeding and had contractions to go to the hospital because I was having a miscarriage. I was not happy, but I felt relieved because I didn't want to marry this man.

Not long after the doctor's visit I began to have severe cramps and bleeding. I was at the movies with my daughter, my friend, and her daughter, while this was happening. After the movie, I sent my daughter home with my friend and went to the hospital. My mother and I were not in a good place at that time, so, I did not bother to call her to let her know that I was in the hospital. I realized later that I was wrong for not letting her know, but I didn't think she cared.

The next day after the procedure, I was discharged. I went to pick up my daughter from my friend's house then I went home. My mother was upset that I didn't let her know that I was in the hospital. She said she was worried about me. I understood why she was upset; however, I was not in the mood for a lecture.

A few months after the miscarriage, I broke it off with my fiancé. My mother was not happy because she wanted me to settle down but, I didn't want to settle. I figured it was my life and I had to choose what was best for me at that time. It was around that time I began to realize that I was still very angry. My mother and I were fighting a lot, which did not help with my anger issues.

One evening after a long day of work and school, I came home and my mom was upset with me for something. I am not even sure what that something was. She started yelling at me calling me all kinds of nasty names. I became so angry and started to curse back at her. She told me to get out. I said, "I am not going anywhere. You made me leave my apartment to come to your house and now you're trying to kick me out."

She called my sister to talk to me. My sister told me to leave to give my mom time to calm down. I said, "I'm not going anywhere with my child at this time." It was after 11 pm, and my mother called the police and told them I threatened to hurt her. I packed a few items in a duffle bag, took my child, and left.

As I was walking outside, I saw police cars and ambulance coming toward the building. I just kept walking; I took a cab to the train station, then I took the train to Brooklyn. I was very angry she made me leave my home to move in with her and now, I was homeless. In my mind, I was never going to speak with her ever again. I went to my sister's house that night to spend the night.

The following day my sister informed me that her father didn't approve of me staying with her and her husband. Her father was judging me because I was a single parent. You can imagine what he thought of me. My sister's husband did not like me, so he did not want me there either. My sister said my daughter could spend the night but I would have to go and come back after her husband left for work the next morning so I could take a shower.

I would sleep on the train then go to my sister's house in the morning to shower and take my daughter to school. I had a very nice lady who babysat my daughter after school so I could go to school. When I went to pick up my daughter from her, I explained my situation to her. I told her I needed a place to stay or leave my daughter for two weeks until I was able to get an apartment. She said she could keep my daughter for two weeks for $200 per week and I could spend one night per week at her house to spend time with my daughter. She was a married woman with four kids of her own. I trusted her because she took good care of my daughter.

I slept on the train and still was going to my sister's house in the morning to shower. Then once a week I would go to the babysitter's house to spend time with my daughter and spend the night there. A friend told me about a basement apartment that was going to be available within those two weeks. I was happy to hear that. I kept in contact with them throughout those two weeks, and everything was going according to plan.

After confirming the apartment was still available for one last time (the day before), I went to pick up my daughter from the babysitter to go to my new apartment. When I arrived at my friend's house, which is the same house that had a basement apartment available, she told me the owner had decided to give the apartment to a family member. I was disappointed as I had no place to stay, and I had my daughter with me.

Thankfully, someone in the area had a studio basement that was going to be available in a couple of days. I went to meet with the owner, and he agreed to let me rent it, I was very excited. But I still needed a place to stay with my daughter for a couple of days until I could move in.

My friend reluctantly asked me to stay at her place for those couple of days. She did it out of guilt. Nonetheless I was relieved because I didn't want to go back to sleeping on the train with my daughter. My friend shared a two-bedroom with her mother and her daughter which meant my friend, her daughter, me, and my daughter had to share a bed. The two girls were in the center, I was on one end and my friend was on the other end.

Something startled me in the middle of the night, and I opened my eyes to see my friend standing over the bed and looking angry. She looked very strange and was mumbling something under her breath. I felt very uncomfortable, When I woke up the next day, I decided that my friend's house was not the best place for me and my daughter.

We rode the train until late at night and then went to a motel for 6 hours to sleep and shower. We did that for a couple of days, then the landlord of the studio basement called to say it was ready. I moved into the studio basement right away. I had to take a leave from school. I was in between jobs. Money was tight.

I did the best I could with what I had. The owner of the house was a single dad in his mid-30s. His son didn't live with him but he visited often. He was a very nice man. He knew I was a struggling young mom and he was very helpful to me. I always shared my dinner with him whenever I cooked, even though I didn't have much. I wanted to show my appreciation for his help.

Chapter Four

PICKING UP THE PIECES

"...he refreshes my soul.
He guides me along the right paths
  for his name's sake."
Psalm 23:3

One day while I was home looking for jobs in the newspaper, I received a phone call from my daughter's grandfather stating that my mom had told him that I was looking for a job. My mom and I were not talking at that time. I am not sure how she knew I was looking for a job, but I was grateful she did. He told me about a receptionist position at his job and gave me all the details and set up an interview for me.

The administrator who conducted the interview was very nice and I thought the interview went well. At the end of the interview, she said the receptionist position had been filled. However, she offered me a position as a dialysis technician. I said, "What is that?" After she explained to me what dialysis was, she asked, "Are you afraid of blood?" She then gave me a tour of the facility; I was fascinated by the way these people were sitting there while their blood was coming out of their bodies. I was intrigued. This was a whole new world that I never knew existed.

Later that day, my daughter's grandfather told me the reason he called me about the job was when he was on the street begging for money, he had asked me for a dollar, and I gave him $10 because I didn't have change. He never forgot about that. You see my daughter's grandfather was an alcoholic. He would go on a two-week drinking binge and beg people on the street for money. When he recovered, he would go back to work and do it again a couple of months later. It was very strange to me. But that's how he lived his life.

After I completed my dialysis training, I received my schedule, and I was on my own. My schedule was a little rough. I worked 4:45 am-6 pm four to six days per week. Since I didn't have reliable transportation, I used to take a cab in the morning. Sometimes the owner of the house where I lived gave me a ride to work.

I worked hard and saved money for a car. I purchased an old 1989 Mazda 929 which lasted a whole six months. Someone cut me off and stopped short during traffic on the belt parkway. My little hooptie was totalled but, I thank God that I was okay. My then boyfriend came to pick me up from the scene of the accident and took me home. I was still very shaky.

He took me to work the next day and whenever he could. He was a good boyfriend at that time. We were together for a total of five years. He lived in Brooklyn in the projects, and I lived in Queens in a studio basement. Three years into the relationship, we discussed living together.

He had a great job with Coca-Cola, and I was making decent money as a dialysis technician. We finally decided to look for a place. We found a beautiful two-bedroom apartment in a convenient area in Brooklyn. I finally felt like life was coming together for me.

Throughout the time we were together my boyfriend and I used to party and drink at least every other weekend. When you're partying, you don't pay attention to how much liquor the other person is consuming, especially if they know how to hold their liquor. While living together I noticed that my boyfriend was drinking heavily daily, I asked him if this was something that he did regularly, and he said yes.

I was taken aback; I never realized that he was a functional alcoholic until we were living together. What is a girl to do? It was difficult watching him destroy his body daily. I was afraid that something bad would happen to him. I wanted him to get help. I attempted to schedule an AA meeting for him, but I was not able to because he had to do it himself. I asked him to schedule it and I promised to go with him but, he refused. He was in denial. I felt so sad for him.

One day after work he was home drinking as usual, and we were arguing about something. He became angry and picked up a football-size heavy glass, like a 3D-shaped glass, and threw it at me. This happened in front of my daughter.

I was terrified. I took my daughter and left that night. He was banging on my car window, trying to block me from leaving. He was making such a scene outside, some of the neighbors came outside to see what was going on. I was mortified. I went back home the following day but I had no intention of staying there with him. I spent all my free time apartment hunting and within a week, I found a basement apartment. My daughter was moving from having her own room to sharing a room with me once again, and I felt terrible.

The following week on my day off, while my boyfriend was at work, I moved out. I made several trips throughout the day with my little car, and by the time it was time to pick up my daughter from school, I had finished moving. I left him a letter expressing how much I cared for him and asked him to get help.

I couldn't stay because that's not the kind of example I was trying to set for my daughter. I wanted to try and help him but my daughter was my priority. He wasn't ready to get help, he was still in denial. I had gone back to school and obtained my degree in business management within that time I was living with him.

My daughter was the only one at my graduation. I felt like nobody cared about me, at least not enough to attend my graduation. After the ceremony, I took my daughter to dinner and a movie. I was sad that no one was able to attend my graduation but I had to be strong for my daughter.

I had a degree in business management. However, I did not know what to do with that degree because I had fallen in love with dialysis and wanted to go to nursing school to be a dialysis nurse. In early 2005 I decided to apply to Adelphi University in the nursing program. I got accepted and was set to start school several months later in August 2005. I was excited about my future. Things started looking up again.

Chapter Five

THE STRUGGLE CONTINUES

"Even though I walk
    through the darkest valley,
I will fear no evil,
    for you are with me;
your rod and your staff,
    they comfort me."
Psalm 23:4

On Mother's Day in May 2005, I was on an online dating site. (I preferred online dating because I liked the idea of getting to know a person before meeting them). While I was on that dating site a man messaged me saying Happy Mother's Day. He sounded very kind, and he was very nice from what I could tell. We communicated online for a little bit and eventually exchanged numbers and then we met in person (in a public place of course).

Things were going great. We spent a lot of time together and I eventually introduced him to my daughter. He used to take us fishing, he took us on our first Disney trip, and we had so much fun together. We spent a lot of time at his house on Long Island. As we were getting to know each other, he expressed the desire to have a baby. He was previously married for 14 years, and he and his ex-wife did not have any children. I wasn't sure that I wanted more kids; however, I was open to the idea.

As the relationship progressed, I began to tell him about some of the traumas that I had experienced when I was younger. We were building a trusting relationship, and he was very kind to my daughter. I loved that he cared about my daughter and that made me care about him more. I had a hectic schedule between school and work, and on the weekends that I worked, he would take my daughter out fishing, to an amusement park, to movies, etc. On the weekends that I was off, we spent most of the time on Long Island with him.

Two years into the relationship he asked me to move in with him. However, I was not ready to take that step. Our relationship was good, and I didn't want to mess things up. I was in my late 20s. I wanted to have my career together before moving in with a man again. He still wanted to have a child with me, and I was not against it but I was not ready. After many conversations, I finally agreed to have a baby with him. The plan was to start working on it after I was done with nursing school. As time went by the relationship became rocky

—we were arguing a lot, and things were going downhill very quickly.

I was very angry with him because he was making light of something that I shared with him that was very traumatic to me. He used to expose himself to me, exactly the way it happened to me with the white man in the elevator. He was a white man also. To him it was like a joke. However, it was not a joke to me. I asked him to stop many times, but he never did. I couldn't understand why he would do this to me, and I became very angry with him. Since he did not respect my wishes and we weren't getting along anyway, I decided to break it off with him.

A week after the breakup, I found out I was pregnant. I didn't know what to do, I had just broken up with him and now I was pregnant. I called him to deliver the news, and neither of us was excited. However, I decided no matter what came out of the conversation, I was going to have my baby. It was summer vacation, and I was due to return to school at the end of summer. I figured I'd be fine going back to school, but my morning sickness was severe—I would be sick the entire day.

At the end of the summer when I was due to return to school, I was admitted to the hospital and was diagnosed with hyperemesis gravidarum. According to the American Pregnancy Association, hyperemesis gravidarum is characterized by severe nausea, vomiting, weight loss, and electrolyte disturbances. Mild cases are treated with dietary changes, rest, and antacids. More severe cases often require a stay in the hospital so that the mother can receive fluid and nutrition through an intravenous line (IV).

Unfortunately, I had a severe case of hyperemesis. I lost 15lbs the first 12 weeks of my pregnancy. I was in and out of the hospital (I was considered a frequent flyer in the hospital). I was always sick. They sent a nurse to my house to put in an IV line so I wouldn't have to go to the hospital so frequently and I could receive IV treatment at home. Because of my small veins, the nurse was unsuccessful in inserting the IV line. I had to be rushed back to the hospital otherwise I would lose my baby.

After I was discharged from the hospital, I went for a follow-up with my GYN doctor, and he advised us to terminate the pregnancy. That was not an option for us, so we eventually changed to a new doctor. Because I was always sick, I couldn't go back to school, and I had to take a leave of absence. My boyfriend and I decided to give our relationship another shot. After all, we had a baby coming. Not that the relationship was great but, we had enough reasons to try and make it work.

My daughter at that time was in her teenage years and we lived in Brooklyn. She attended summer camp and sometimes she would go home, and I would be in the hospital. It was difficult for me to take care of her. I was either in the hospital or at home in bed sick.

My boyfriend once again asked me to move in with him. He had a live-in housekeeper which was very helpful to us. I reluctantly moved in with him. It was nice to see my daughter finally having her own space again as we had been sharing a room for most of her life. He used to take her to activities while I was at home sick; he was very good to her. And that is one of the main reasons I stayed with him.

One day while I was in my room resting, I heard my daughter arguing with my boyfriend about something and they were both mad and yelling at each other. He shouted, "Nobody speaks to me like that in my house." I wasn't expecting that from him. While I understood it wasn't my house, I thought we were making it our home. I was expecting him to come and talk to me about whatever was going on. From that day on I was on guard and planning my way out of his house.

My pregnancy was very tough, and my boyfriend was very uncooperative. I would send him to get me something that I was craving, and he would return with something else that I did not ask for. I would get so angry, I had explained to him many times that if I asked for something I was craving, he needed to get the exact thing I asked for. Even my daughter tried to explain to him but, he refused to understand.

He took everything so personally. Eventually, he started to compare me to his best friend's wife, saying "So and so's wife was not like that when she was pregnant." He had no understanding of what I was going through. I was so miserable and lonely. Sometimes I felt like he just didn't care. I spent most of my pregnancy fighting with him. There were times when my daughter and I left the house and spent the night in a hotel room just to have peace.

After 9 months of misery, I finally gave birth to a beautiful 9lb healthy baby boy. I was excited to be his mom. After giving birth, his father was very controlling and did not want any family members to visit me. I craved those visits because I was lonely. My boyfriend was chasing everyone away. He did not want me to have any company in the house.

I had the baby blues the first two weeks after giving birth and my son's father trying to control everything wasn't much help. He insisted that I was depressed and needed to see somebody right away. I tried to explain to him that the baby blues was normal after giving birth. He insisted on taking me to the doctor anyway. I obliged because I really couldn't tolerate him complaining and telling everyone that I was depressed. We went to the doctor, and after my assessment, the doctor said I was fine, but he refused to believe the doctor.

He continued telling everyone that I was going through post-partum depression. It was very frustrating to me. At that point, I checked out of the relationship completely. He was not respecting me as a human being and that was very upsetting to me. I took an additional six months off from school to bond with my baby and when I did go back to school, I went part-time for the first semester.

My relationship with my son's father was on shaky ground. I had some resentment for the way he treated me when I was pregnant and the way he was treating me since giving birth. He was pressuring me to lose the baby weight again saying so and so's wife lost the weight fast. His nagging made me angry. I eventually told him to go be with So and so's wife.

Another thing that I found upsetting was him introducing me as Minie. He assumed that his friends wouldn't be able to pronounce my name, so he just shortened it. I hated being called Minie. No matter how many times I explained to him to not introduce me as Minie, he never listened, and this was very frustrating for me.

I was back to school full-time and was doing my clinical rotation in the hospital. When I went back home my son's father always asked if the doctors were flirting with me and questioned me about my day in a jealous way. Then shortly after I went back to school he began to talk about marriage. He seemed in a hurry to get married. He wanted to get married before I was done with nursing school. He said I didn't have to go to school or work because he would take care of us.

What he didn't realize was that I was going to school for myself. I wanted to accomplish something for myself and my children. I told him that I would marry him after I was done with school. He was not happy about that however, we agreed on me wearing the ring to appear unavailable to other men. I was okay with that because my priority at that time was to finish nursing school.

Every day was a different argument, I found myself going to the guest room to study. He knew if I failed two nursing classes I would be kicked out of the nursing program. I felt like he was trying to get me kicked out of the nursing program so he could have what he wanted, a stay-at-home wife. If anyone was kicked out of the nursing program, they would have to wait another three years to become eligible to re-apply to any nursing school. And they would still be responsible to pay for whatever student loans they had been granted before being kicked out of the program. I didn't want that to happen to me.

Despite all the studying I had done, I ended up failing a class. I was devastated, even though I had another chance to take it again, I was afraid that I would fail it again. I had to figure something out quickly. During an argument, I told him that I failed because he always started a fight to distract me from my studies. He said, "No. You failed because YOU'RE STUPID." I was deeply hurt; I was already filled with doubt and now he was saying that I was stupid. I decided that this relationship was not going to work for me. I did not need to be in a relationship with someone who did not respect me and was verbally abusive to me.

People and family members advised me to stay with him because we shared a child. I didn't want my children to watch me get verbally abused by someone who was supposed to love me. That crushed my spirit but, I was not going to allow this to break me. I was not a stranger to struggling except this time I would be struggling with two kids. I was almost done with nursing school; I knew my struggle would be for a short period this time. I was already working a per diem job as a dialysis technician, I applied for a second per diem job.

I was not trying to take time off from school again. I started looking for an apartment. I figured if I found something close by it would make things easier for our son. After a couple of weeks of apartment hunting, I found a one-bedroom apartment nearby—it was practically in the attic. The couple renting the apartment was very nice. After meeting with them and talking for a while, they decided to take $100 off the rent. I'm not sure why because I didn't tell them about my situation. But I was grateful that they took $100 off.

That day I went home and told my son's father I was moving out; he made a big scene saying I was trying to take his son away from him. He was so dramatic. He was upset because he assumed that I was moving back to Brooklyn with our son. I did want to move back to Brooklyn; however, things would have been much harder for me in Brooklyn. My daughter was already in the Long Island school system, I had been moving around with her for the past couple of years, and I was not going to do that to her again.

I gave him the address and told him it was 3 minutes away from where he lived. On moving day, I packed my little car and made a couple of trips to get all my belongings into the new place. In the new apartment, I shared the room with my son while my daughter slept in the living room. I wanted to work out a schedule for my son with his dad however, his father was not on board. I had to retain an attorney because he was trying to paint an ugly picture of me. He was very bitter and angry. We finally went to court and got a schedule for our son.

We were getting along fine at times and not so well at other times; it was always a blowout full of insults at each other. But I did not let that distract me from my goal. He had to pay child support; he wasn't excited about that at all. He would take me to court for every little thing. I had so much anger towards him because I felt like his life purpose was to torture me. He was never happy with anything. I always had to give in because I had to reach my goal, and I didn't want these little distractions to interfere with my future.

I had to take on another per diem job to work every other weekend to make ends meet. My schoolwork was now at risk because I didn't have enough time to study. I found out that I was failing another class. I was devastated but I had enough time to turn things around. I went to talk to the professor to find out what I needed to pass this class. I waited in the hallway as the professor was finishing up with another student. As the student was walking out of the professor's office she began to cry.

Now I was terrified to go and speak with her. During the meeting, I learned that I needed to have at least 90% in the last two exams and have the full 10% of a required test called ATI to pass the class. I didn't know how I was going to do it but, I was not going to stop trying. As soon as I got home, I emailed that student who walked out crying and said to her "It looks like we are both struggling in this class. Would you like to get together and figure out how we're going to pass?" She responded within 24 hours and we met at the school library the following day to hatch out a plan. We devoted every minute of our free time to a private room in the school library to study and test each other.

Whenever it was my son's father's turn to have him overnight, I would be at the school library until closing time. We took one of the two exams; I made it in the high 80s but not 90% which meant I would have to do better than a 90% in the final exam to pass the class. I was praying and worshiping daily, I knew God had a great plan for my life and I was not going to let anything, or anyone stop me.

I had to pause on one of the per diem jobs for a few weeks so I could study for the final and the ATI. Now it was time to take the ATI. Everyone had the opportunity to take the ATI test twice, and the points would be added up to get a total of 10%. I took it the first time and had 7%, I didn't panic because I knew I had another chance to get the remaining 3%. I took it the second time and I got the 3% to make a total of 10%.

Unfortunately, the other student did not make the 10%. She would need an even higher score in the final to pass the class. Days before the final we met in the school library every day, either morning or afternoon. On the day of the final, we had some time to review as the final was in the afternoon. We met at the school library, reviewed our notes, tested each other, and then we went for our final exam.

I passed with 98% and made it through. I was on cloud nine. Unfortunately, the other student did not score high enough to pass the class, resulting in her being kicked out of the nursing program. It was bittersweet for me—I was happy for myself but sad for her. It was difficult for both of us to keep in touch, but we remained Facebook friends and a couple of years later she was able to attend nursing school and graduated. I believe God sent her to help me get through that class. It was God's plan for me.

Chapter Six

A GLIMMER OF LIGHT

"You prepare a table before me
Psalm 23:5a

After two years and a half in school following the birth of my son, I finally graduated from nursing school. This time, my mother, my little sister, my godmother, my children, and even my son's father were able to attend my graduation to cheer me on. I received the perseverance award during my pinning ceremony. I had a professor that I trusted enough to talk to her about my life and what was going on at home.

Around that time, I had a cancer scare (with my thyroid), and she was a great support system for me. She nominated me for the Perseverance Award. I was not expecting any awards. Just graduating was a good enough accomplishment for me; the award was the icing on the cake. I was very happy, and my family was happy for me. I thought to myself, I am finally making my mother proud, after all the years of embarrassment and shame.

I am sure she has always been proud of me; however, it never felt that way to me. Maybe it was my own shame that made me feel that way. After graduation, I had to set aside time to study for my nursing license exam. One of my classmates and I decided to review together for our exam. We attended a review course for two weeks and set aside an additional 4 weeks to review on our own. We decided to schedule the test 6 weeks after graduation.

I locked myself in the house. I only went out to work and to spend time with my son. My daughter was about 17 years old, and the last thing she wanted was to spend time with me. I spent all my time studying, fasting, and praying. One day while I was taking a break I sat on the couch and fell asleep; I had a clear vision of God speaking to me telling me I was going to pass the boards.

I woke up motivated and happy because I knew then I was going to pass. I continued to study, fasting and praying. The day before the test I fasted and prayed. I didn't study that day. Instead, I just reviewed the lab values, and I felt calm and at peace. The only person who knew I was taking the test was that one classmate that I was studying with. On the day of the test, I woke up early to pray and meditate on God's word, and then I went to the test facility.

I went early to avoid traffic or anything that would affect me getting there on time. I got there, parked my car, worshiped, and prayed for another 30 minutes then I went inside 30 minutes before the time I was supposed to be there. The test was 265 questions and we had 6 hours to complete it. The computer could stop at 75 questions if you were doing very well or very poorly. I sat for my test and began to answer the questions, after 80 questions I raised my hand to go to the restroom. When I returned from the restroom, I answered one more question, and then the computer screen turned blue.

I began to panic and raised my hand; the lady came over and said that I was done with my test. I wasn't surprised. I was wondering whether I did well or bad but inside I felt like I did well. God has never failed me; He has always kept His word. I decided to wait for the result before telling anyone. After the test, I went to pick up my son from his father's house and his father asked me what was so important that I needed him to watch our son. Then he asked, "Was your test today?" I didn't want to tell him, but I didn't want to lie, so I told him not to tell anyone.

The test was on a Friday, we had to wait until Sunday to get the result. I kept myself occupied. I was scheduled to work all day that Saturday, and I went to work. Everyone kept asking when I was going to take my test, I responded that I would let them know when it is done. On Sunday morning, I woke up early to look for my result. I went online, and the website was under their monthly maintenance until the afternoon.

I went to church, then after church, I went straight home. I went on my computer and there it was, the one word I was waiting for: "PASSED!" I was excited. I called my mother and said, "Hello this is Minoude the RN," and my mother was screaming with joy. We were all so happy. Finally, I felt accomplished.

Now, it was time to get a nursing job. I was working for a company in Brooklyn when I was a dialysis technician. The administrator was good to me for the most part. I contacted him and told him that I was a nurse and was looking for work. He invited me for an interview with the clinic manager. I went in for the interview and met the clinic manager and the team. I saw people I used to work with when I was a dialysis technician, and I felt at home. The manager offered me the position, and the administrator and I negotiated a salary and agreed on a start date.

I was a new nurse who needed to be trained. Training was not a challenge because I had been a dialysis technician for ten years; I just needed to learn the nursing part. When I received my first paycheck, I noticed my hourly rate was different than what was discussed. I contacted the administrator to find out what happened. He told me that the facility was new, and they were not making enough money yet and he asked me to bear with him. I told him he should have discussed this with me beforehand. I was driving about 1-1.5 hours to Brooklyn from Long Island for this job, and they didn't have parking.

I wish he had told me in the beginning. I wanted to save money to move out of the attic apartment, and with the cut in salary, it would be challenging for me. I began to look for jobs in Long Island, even if the pay was the same as in Brooklyn. I would be spending less money on gas and less wear and tear on my little hooptie.

Three months later I found a job closer to home with better pay. I went to the administrator and told him about my new job and handed in my resignation letter. He asked me to stay on as per diem and I agreed after discussing a per diem rate. I was going to Brooklyn at least once per week to work as per diem, and when I received my check, the same thing happened again, he did not pay me the rate we discussed and agreed on. I eventually asked him to take me off his schedule; it was not worth all the trouble.

A few months into the new job I started to save money to move out of the attic apartment. In those same few months, I was summoned to court by my son's father. He reported to the court that I was a nurse now, making double his salary, and needed to reduce child support. I graduated with a $95,000 student loan to pay back, two kids, and living in an attic apartment, trying to put money together for a bigger apartment.

My son's father has his own business, his own house which is paid in full, and he was making close to half a million dollars a year (he had told me in the past when he wanted me to quit school to be a housewife). This is the same man who asked me to quit school and work and he would take care of me and my children. He went to court and showed that his personal income was only $35,000 annually.

I didn't want to fight about this because he and I both knew he was lying, and I could not afford to retain an attorney to go through all the discoveries. I just gave in and let him have it, I was tired of fighting. The judge reduced the child support by greater than 50%. I had come to realize that no matter what happened or what I am going through, God has always provided, and I knew that He will always provide for me.

I had been going to church all my life, and back in the early 2000s when I was working as a dialysis technician, I began to attend a church in Valley Stream located across the street from my job. Even after I left that job, I continued to go to that church with my kids. After reflecting on all that God had done for me throughout the years and how he protected me from harm, I decided to give my life to Christ. I got water baptized in early 2011 and began to attend different classes in the church to help me grow in my Christian walk.

Since I had my son, I have only claimed tax with him once, in his first year. His father has always been the one claiming him year after year. He has not asked if I wanted to file with my son nor did he offer to split whatever he receives for my son with me. When my son was 6 years old, I told him I needed to file with my son. I thought I was going to end up owing the IRS. He did not say no however, he went ahead and filed with my son without my knowledge.

I too filed with my son because he did not say I couldn't, I was audited by the IRS. Thankfully, he hadn't paid child support for over a year at that time, I took him to court and the judge made him pay me all the back child support. I used that back child support money to pay back the IRS.

There was a stipulation in our initial custody agreement that I could not move more than 15 miles from where my son's father lived. I found a beautiful apartment in Valley Stream; it was about 17 miles away. I had to go to court to make sure it was okay for me to move there, as my son's father was making it a big deal. The judge said I could move; however, I would be responsible for bringing my son to Farmingdale for his visits with his dad. His dad and I agreed about keeping him in the Farmingdale school district since he had already started school there. I had no problem with getting my son to school and back.

Things were going well at work. However, there were not many opportunities for growth in that facility. It was a union job; one would have to work ten years before they could be in charge and then many more years to be a manager. I started looking for a new position with a growth opportunity.

My church was doing their annual corporate fast. I joined the fast, and even led a small group at my house for the fast. I prayed and asked God to help me get a position with growth opportunity. Within those twenty-one days I was applying for jobs and finally, someone contacted me to schedule an interview. The night before the interview, I had a vision of the place where I was going to be working. I went to the interview, and everything went well. The administrator asked if I wanted to see the treatment area. I said yes, and when she opened the door, it was the exact replica of what I saw in my vision the night before. I was amazed, and she said, "Somebody you've worked with in the past referred you to me; this meeting was just a formality." Look at God; He has always been faithful to me.

I was excited to start my new position, but the nurses working there were mean and nasty. All my nursing career there was a saying that nurses eat their young. Well, I can finally confirm that this is a true statement. Even though the nurses were mean and nasty, I was not intimidated by any of them. I remember an incident with a patient where the patient was passing out or cramping and the nurse assigned to that patient had stepped out. I went to assist the patient and then documented what I did. When that nurse came back, she said to me "Who told you to assist my patient?"

I said, "I did not realize you had personal patients; my understanding is every patient in this facility is our patient," then I walked away. Those nurses tried and tested me but I always stood my ground. Within ninety days of being in that facility, only one of the two nurses made it, the other one was terminated. And within those same ninety days, I was the nurse in charge and that other nurse was taking orders from me. Do you see how God works? It was a good reminder to treat people well.

Two years into that position I was promoted to nurse manager. In December 2013, I learned my then 20-year-old daughter was pregnant. I was living in a beautiful 2-bedroom apartment in Valley Stream. I wanted to stay there forever but it was not enough space to bring in another child.

I was doing better financially, and the housing market was great for buyers. I decided to buy a house; we needed the space for the baby anyway. After months of house hunting, we finally found a house in West Babylon within my budget. Everything went smoothly; we moved into the house three months before my daughter was due to give birth. Close to my daughter giving birth, I began to feel like something was wrong. I reached out to my pastor and asked him to pray for my daughter and her baby. When we went to the hospital everything was going well, and then suddenly, the baby was not getting enough oxygen; they had to do an emergency c-section. My daughter gave birth to a beautiful healthy eight-pound girl. I was excited, even though she made me a grandmother at the tender age of 37.

Things were a little tough because I now had a mortgage and other bills. However, I was happy having my own home. When my granddaughter was one and a half years old, my daughter started going back to the life she led before having a baby. It wasn't great; I don't want to share details about her life because this book is about my life, not hers. She started hanging out with the wrong crowd again.

I was struggling with the mortgage, living paycheck to paycheck, and using my credit card to the max. I had gotten a per diem job to help keep my head above water. I asked my daughter to pay a bill or pay $500 per month for the house bills. She was working, she had a car, childcare was free for her, and I was willing to negotiate with her if she couldn't manage to pay $500. She asked, "What happens if I don't pay?" I said, "You will have to find another place to stay."

My daughter and I weren't getting along at that time, so she decided to move out and stay at a friend's house with her daughter. After two weeks of staying with her friend and family, they told her she couldn't stay there anymore. She then moved to a family shelter. I believe my daughter did all that to show me that she could do it on her own. Unfortunately, she couldn't.

I was still seeing my granddaughter almost every day, but my granddaughter was not allowed to stay overnight. At some point during her stay in the shelter, my daughter decided that she wanted to party and not be a responsible mother. She started leaving my granddaughter with friends while she was out partying. I had a problem with her leaving my granddaughter with friends.

Eventually, my daughter asked me to take my granddaughter for a little while. I agreed to take her, however, I wanted to do it legally so that my granddaughter could be under my insurance, and I would be able to enroll her in school. We went to family court, and we agreed that I would have custody of my granddaughter as of June 2017.

Before getting custody of my granddaughter, I was dating a man for a few months. I believe when you are going through a tough time, you don't always see clearly and that's what happened with me and this man. He appeared decent and had a lot to offer. A few months into the relationship, he started talking about moving to Florida. I did like the idea of moving to Florida because I needed a break; I felt stuck. I purchased the house to accommodate my daughter and my granddaughter and now I was left in the house with my son whom I shared custody with his father. I didn't have him every day, and my granddaughter was now with me full time, and the bills were piling up.

After much thought and consideration, I decided I was going to move to Florida with him. Before I knew it, we were getting my house ready to put on the market. He fixed a few things and rearranged the furniture to make the house look more spacious. He did a really good job. I was ready to move to Florida, but now I had to break the news to my family. I talked about it with my son, and we agreed that he would come after he was done with elementary school. He was in the 5th grade and had a few months to go.

Before I could tell his father, my son told him. His father said I could not take his son to Florida. The reason I spoke with my son first is if my son was not onboard, I wouldn't have moved forward with my plans.

Now it was time to tell my mom and the rest of the family. Nobody understood what I was doing because they had no idea of what I was going through. This man I was moving with had one child of his own and 2 stepchildren from a previous relationship. We were all going to live in this big house he had on the golf course.

I was okay with it; however, I had a plan B for when my son came to live with me. I had planned on going to court because I was moving before my son was done with school and knowing his father, he might accuse me of abandoning my son. We went to court to modify the custody agreement. When we were in front of the judge, my son's father was with his attorney, I didn't hire an attorney since we had agreed on everything prior.

His attorney had drawn some paper per his request to present to the court. In this document, he was saying such nasty things about me. Fortunately, the judge threw it out of court because I had filed my petition to modify the custody first. I had secured a nursing position in Florida, I got a license to practice in Florida, and I was almost all set to go. Until I saw a paper of divorce proceeding for my boyfriend. I was confused because this man had told me that he was divorced. When I confronted him about it, he told me it was not finalized but not to worry, it was a matter of time. Since I had my agenda anyway, I went ahead with the plans.

My house took longer than expected to sell because the buyer got sick and things prolonged due to his sickness. Finally, in October 2017 my house sold, and I made a profit and paid all my bills right before moving to Florida. I moved on October 30th, 2017. I knew I hated being in Florida the first week I was there. However, I didn't have all the struggles that I was experiencing in NY.

I cried every day; I missed my son and my family. Whenever I was on the phone with my son, his father would be there in the background talking to my son while my son was talking to me. His father supervised every call. At times it felt like my son didn't want to talk to me, but it was because his father would not allow him to have a little privacy while talking to me.

Shortly after arriving in Florida, I moved out of my boyfriend's house into my own place because I wanted my own space for when my kids came to visit. When it was my weekend with my son, his father refused to let him fly to Florida alone. I had to fly to NY with my granddaughter to pick up my son for the weekend. Most of the time I spent the weekend in NY because it was more convenient. I was flying to NY every other weekend to pick up my son.

My son's father and I were fighting daily; he couldn't understand why I left, and he was trying to punish me for leaving. When my son got to Florida, he told me he was not happy staying with his dad who always threatened to take away his things, specifically his phone so he wouldn't be able to talk to me. He said when he talked back or questioned his dad about anything, his dad told him, "You're acting like your mom." My heart broke listening to the things that my son was saying to me.

I knew from that conversation, I had to move back to NY so I began to look for work in NY. Shortly after I found a position I was interested in, they contacted me and scheduled a phone interview, followed by an in-person interview the following week. I scheduled my interview for a Friday so I could spend the rest of the weekend in NY with my son since it was my weekend to have him. The interview went well; right away she offered me the position and I accepted. The job was in Brooklyn, a little further than I would have liked. I figured once I settle in NY, I could get a job closer to home.

My manager in Florida was very understanding as she witnessed the fights I was having with my son's father and all the traveling back and forth to NY and she accommodated me once to attend court in the office. I flew to NY one last time to finalize paperwork with the new position and picked up my son for Spring break. I had already decided to stay at my mom's house, and I left my granddaughter in NY with my mom for a week while my son and I flew back to Florida.

My son and I packed my car with as much as we could fit in it and drove back to NY. I had to pay extra for getting out of my lease 8 months early and I gave away all my furniture and other items that could not fit in my car. While we were on the road driving back to NY, we spent a couple of days exploring different cities; we had a wonderful time.

Chapter Seven

ONE LAST FIGHT

"...in the presence of my enemies."
Psalm 23:5b

*N*ow that I was back in NY, I had to get the custody agreement revised to have more time with my son during the week. I retained an attorney; I was expecting to have an equal amount of time as his father (50/50). My savings account was good, even though I was flying to NY frequently, I was still able to save, plus I had some of the profit I made from selling my house.

We went to court, which I was expecting it to be easy, but I was wrong. We were battling in court for almost a year because I refused to give in to him this time. I knew I was not about to give up on my son. Then finally one day, his friend died by suicide. He texted me to tell me what happened, and he was very sad about it. A week later he called me and said, "I don't want to fight anymore; you can have whatever you want and by the way, I will also stop taking child support." I said I needed this in writing. He said he was going to contact his attorney.

Later that day his attorney sent me a custody agreement via email. However, it was not 50/50. I called him asking him what kind of games he was playing. He apologized and said he was going to call his attorney and have her make the corrections. Finally, she emailed me the custody agreement; it was 50/50. I was not relieved because I did not trust him; we were due in court in two weeks. I spent those two weeks praying and asking God for strength in case he decided to change his mind last minute. Before the court, I had moved to an apartment close to my son's school to show the judge that I wasn't playing around.

When we got to court, as I was stating my name and new address, I saw the stenographer shaking her head in a way that made me feel as if she agreed with me moving closer to my son's school. I felt a little relieved. Shortly after, the judge asked us if we had an agreement. We said yes and it was read in the court. We agreed, and it was done.

Next, we needed to go to court for child support. I was thinking that now that I was paying rent and my credit cards were maxed out, he needed to keep his word. When the time came, we went to the court. Of course I brought my attorney. We were sworn in, and he told the judge he wanted to stop the child support. The judge said, "Are you sure?" Even though we had 50/50 custody the person who makes more money can still be required to pay a percentage of child support. He replied, "I understand and it's fine." Finally, I was relieved.

Chapter Eight

FORGIVENESS

"You anoint my head with oil;"
Psalm 23:5c

*W*e have all heard the saying hurt people, hurt people. I did not realize how hurt I was. In my mind everyone hurt me. However, I never realized that I played a part in it as well. I was carrying the pain from my childhood in every relationship, not realizing that I needed to heal before I could have a healthy relationship. I craved to feel loved by anyone, not realizing that I needed to love myself first. I thank God for His love and how He has shown me how much I am loved by Him. Once I realized truly how much God loves me, it gave me all the strength I needed to love myself and share my love with others.

My therapist sent me a forgiveness questionnaire, which was very helpful in the process of forgiveness. It took me some time to forgive my son's father. I had to understand what his childhood was like to understand why he treated me the way he did. I can now say I have completely forgiven my son's father, and I thank God for that. I had always forgiven my mother. Out of ten children, my mother is the only one who did anything to make a better life for her family. Without her sacrifice, I wouldn't be here. Not only did she make a better life for me and my sisters, but she also made a better life for her entire family. They are all thriving in the U.S. because of my mother. My mother is the matriarch of the family. Everything she did, she did for us, and she did it with a third-grade education. I am beyond proud of her, and I will do anything for her.

It took some time to forgive my father for rejecting me. I am not sure that I had fully forgiven him until recently. I always helped him financially; however, I stopped calling him and I didn't always answer when he called. I felt like he was never calling to see how I was doing; he was mainly calling to ask for money. I would just give the money to my mother to send to him. In the end, I stopped all communication with him because I was still upset that he only called when he needed something. On June 17, 2022, my brother sent a message to say that my father had passed away. At first, I was angry at my father because he never acknowledged his wrongdoing. But then I had to give it to God and ask Him to help me to forgive my father and that's when I was able to forgive him and mourn his death. I am now at peace with everything.

As for my abusive aunt, she came to the United States 13 years ago and the minute I saw her I noticed a difference in her. She was so kind and sweet; I forgave her right away. After giving it some thought I realized that my aunt was in her 20's when she had to take care of us —only God knows what she was dealing with. I remember in my 20's even though I was already a mother, I was not in a place to take care of any kids. My aunt did not have any children of her own, but as a child, I did not have the understanding. As I matured, I realized there is a reason for everything. I am not excusing abuse, but I now understand better.

Chapter Nine

WHAT IN THE WORLD?

"...my cup overflows." Psalm 23:5c

*I*n March 2020, the world was shut down due to the Covid 19 pandemic; the school was shut down and I was required to go to work and teach my granddaughter and my son at home. It was a difficult time for me because God was still working on my patience. The apartment that I lived in suddenly felt small. I lived in a 2-bedroom house with my son and my granddaughter. I was sharing a room with my grand-daughter. They were home all day, and my son's father and I had to work together to ensure that everything was smooth with home school.

I was working, coming home frustrated at times because my patients were dying from Covid. It was tough. My lease was ending on December 2020 and the owner of the house contacted me to ask if I was staying. I liked the area, but I didn't have enough space. He asked what my plan was, and I told him I was looking for a bigger space. He asked about my budget and exactly what I was looking for. I answered all his questions and didn't think anything of it.

A week later he called me, and said, "You are a good tenant, and I don't want to lose you. I just bought a house nearby. Here's the address in the area; renovation will take 6-8 weeks. Go see it and let me know what you think." It was 2 minutes from where I lived. I went inside and he showed me everything; it was three bedrooms, and two baths. I was just happy that I was finally going to have my own bathroom once again. On February 2021 I moved into the new place, and it has been great for me and the kids.

When the pandemic started, I began attending church online. One day while watching online I saw that one of our pastors was moving to a church nearby as the lead pastor. I was happy for him. I said to myself, "I will visit him one day." That one day finally came in July 2021—I went to Freedom Chapel for a visit, then I went back the following Sunday. And kept on going. I felt God telling me that this was my home church.

I met a woman whom I was friendly with at the previous church. She and I talked for a little bit and exchanged numbers. The following week we met after church and chatted some more then she introduced me to a couple of women of God. At some point in the conversation, I had expressed to her my desire to be in the church drama/dance team. She encouraged me to meet with the person in charge. The following week I was due to speak with the person in charge but, I avoided her a couple of times until I was ready to go home, and God brought her directly in front of me. I said, "Alright Lord, you got me," and I spoke to her; she invited me to rehearsal to see what they were working on at that time. I was happy and nervous because I wasn't sure of what I was getting myself into.

A few months down the line I participated in the Easter production, and it was during the rehearsals I began to connect with more people in the church and build friendships. I am now feeling like I am living the life God intended for me. I have always put my life aside to care for my children. I didn't have lasting friendships because my time was devoted to my work and my kids. I feel like God has even bigger plans for my life. I can feel it. God is stirring something up in me; this is the first time that I feel alive, and I love it.

I have met two beautiful women of God at my church and our relationship quickly developed into a beautiful friendship. They are like my little sisters; they have such beautiful souls. These two beautiful young ladies were there for me when my father passed away. They came to my house with food and spent the entire day with me encouraging me. They blessed me; I am grateful that they were there to support me in my time of need. Unfortunately, one of the friendships didn't last long but, I believe God placed her in my life for that season and I am grateful.

In Spring 2022, my daughter announced that she was ready to take her daughter back; I was very sad. I knew the day was coming; however, I didn't expect it for a couple more years. I didn't know what I was going to do as my whole life revolved around my son and my grand-daughter. A few weeks after my granddaughter moved back with her mom, I was moping around the house not knowing what I wanted to do. I finally had some time to myself, and I wasn't happy because I missed her so much.

Finally, one day I decided to pick myself up and figure out my life. This time alone made me realize that I was no longer fulfilled as a dialysis nurse manager. I wanted to try other areas in nursing. I truly wanted to open a med spa. However, I was not equipped to do so on my own at the time. I continued working as a nurse manager realizing I was not happy where I was. I decided in December 2022 to quit my job as a dialysis nurse manager even though I had no solid plan or another position to fall back on.

In passing I mentioned to my sister that we should do business together. She is a business owner, and we are both trained in body sculpting. As a nurse, I can offer other services. It was a great idea, but I never sought God about this decision, and this was a decision made on a whim. After a few rejections on rental places, I went to God asking, "Why we are being rejected by places that we can afford? We have had good credit." That's when God revealed to me that He was not in agreement with me doing business with my sister at this time. My sister is a Christian. However, my sister also enjoys being in the world. God revealed to me that He would not be able to fully bless me if I went into business with my sister. I am back in the workforce working as a Home Infusion Nurse Specialist until God makes His move.

Chapter Ten

MY RELATIONSHIPS

"Surely your goodness and love will follow me
all the days of my life."
Psalm 23:6a

My relationship with my daughter has been very challenging in the past; she and I didn't get along for many years. Our relationship was very volatile; one day we were okay and the next we were at each other's throats. Our relationship got better when she was pregnant with her first child—we got along great, and we did a lot of activities together.

A year or so after my granddaughter was born, my daughter decided to go back to her old ways. I was extremely disappointed, and we spent many years fighting. As I began to do some soul searching, I realized that my daughter was acting out because of our life circumstances. I never considered her feelings; I thought everything that I did, I did for her. In my mind, I thought she should be grateful because I tried to give her everything.

I watched several young ladies in the group home partying, doing drugs, even getting their children taken away from them. I expected my daughter to be grateful that I was a good parent to her, and that I sacrificed everything for her. I never realized how growing up without a father had affected my daughter. I thought I did everything to fill in that gap. I was very harsh with my daughter; I felt like she didn't appreciate anything that I did for her.

I never understood her behavior until I got older, and it was after my own father rejected me that I realized that maybe my daughter behaved the way she did because she needed her father. I practically grew up without both my parents, and I never realized how deeply I was affected by it. I understood why my mom traveled a lot because had she not traveled to make a better life for me and my sister, I don't know where I would be. My father lived in Haiti when I was in Haiti and still, he made no effort to spend time with me. I never stopped to think that my daughter needed her father because she had me. I was wrong.

I had no one to help me realize that my daughter needed her dad; everyone in my life was so busy complimenting me as a mom that I didn't stop to think about what it was like for her. The good news is that now that my daughter is a mother of three, she has a better understanding of what I have gone through. We were able to have small conversations about the past at one point, but nothing too deep yet. She did get in touch with her dad and realized that a relationship with him was not all that it was cracked up to be. Unfortunately, my daughter and I still do not see eye to eye on things. I recently had to release her and hope that one day we can resolve our issues.

My son and I are great. He is not perfect; however, I can have conversations with him where he understands and forgives. I had to have a conversation with him about me moving to Florida. I had a revelation that I needed to apologize to him for moving to Florida and putting him in the middle of an adult conversation. I had no right to talk to him about moving to Florida; he was only nine years old. When it happened, I was so desperate to get out of my situation that I was not thinking clearly. I am not afraid to own my mistakes and apologize for them and my son understood and forgave me. I thank God for His revelation.

My sisters and I get along great; I would have liked a closer relationship with my sisters. Unfortunately, we are all very different. I was raised with my older sister until I was around fourteen years old. However, my little sister and I were not raised in the same household. I was thirteen years old when she was born, and I left my mom's house when I was 14 years old. I spent time with her when she was younger, however, we did not always get along. Thank God that we do get along much better now that we are both older and wiser. I love my sisters and would do anything for them. However, I don't think we have that sisterly bond. I still have hope that we will grow closer to one another; it's never too late.

As for my son's father, it is still a work in progress. He doesn't always follow or respect my boundaries but, I am still praying that God continues to work in me, so I don't lose my focus. We do get along but it's a day-to-day process. I have learned to set boundaries with him and repeat myself when I need to. I have learned to forgive, and I don't want to hold on to past hurts. I know that God has blessed me, and He also wants to do a great work in me. I do pray for him always that God will do a work in him as well; nothing is impossible with God.

LOOKING AHEAD

"and I will dwell in the house of the Lord
forever."
Psalm 23:6b

Twenty-Twenty-two (2022) was a great year for me. Even though my granddaughter no longer lives with me, it made me realize that I was made for more. In early 2023 I enrolled in Bible school, and I met this beautiful woman of God who loved on me, and we became great friends. We are now a part of each other's family. I am so grateful to God for putting us together as friends and I can't wait to see what the future holds.

I am waiting on God's perfect timing for my husband. I know if He says it, He will do it. I continue to surrender to His will daily and when I fall short, I ask for forgiveness. I desire to please God; everything I do is spirit-led. I have learned to live in the spirit and not in the flesh and when I get fleshy, I ask God to forgive and help me to get back on track.

AFTERWORD

The process of writing this book has been such an emotional roller coaster for me. I had to re-live all the trauma that I had experienced as a young child. Sometimes I asked God why he was putting me through this torture again. I knew it was to help me heal. However, it did not feel that way at the time.

I am happy that I sought professional help but after prayer and fasting God revealed to me that I was still harboring some resentment and unforgiveness toward my son's father. I thought I had forgiven him a long time ago. What I realized was that I let things go because he is the father of my child and I must interact with him, at least until my son is eighteen years old.

I swept everything under the rug and did not deal with the hurt and the pain that he caused me. God was not going to let me move forward to another relationship without dealing with this first, so I surrendered. And

now I am completely free and at peace. Thank you,
Jesus!

ABOUT THE AUTHOR

Minoude was born in Haiti on October 27, 1977, and arrived in the United States when she was twelve years old. She completed most of her education in New York. Minoude graduated from Adelphi University with a Bachelor of Science and has since worked as a Registered Professional Nurse for fourteen years. Minoude spent most of her career working in dialysis, she was a dialysis technician for ten years before she became a nurse. She currently works as a Home Care Infusion Registered Nurse Specialist and enjoys every opportunity to meet and care for patients. Minoude enjoys spending time with her friends and family doing various activities including dinner, prayer meetings, bowling shopping, and rollerblading. Minoude's favorite activity is rollerblading in the park, on the trail or wherever she finds smooth ground.

God blessed Minoude with her husband Alexander Lewis in February 2024. She continues to enjoy life while encouraging others experiencing difficulties similar to what she previously experienced to trust God who never fails. God has shown Himself mighty in Minoude's life, her prayer is that He will do the same for all of you. Many blessings!